HELP! I Threw Out My Back!

Four Workouts to
Ease Muscle Tension and
Develop Core Strength

Chris Janke-Bueno

Photography by Alison Williams

CHRIS JANKE-BUENO

ISBN: 9781797651767

DEDICATION

This book is dedicated to my dear grandfather. Geetz, I know you're still here with me. I love you.

THANK YOU

Thank you to all my clients, for your support and encouragement. Thanks to my editors: mom, Katie, Amor, and everyone else who gave me feedback for this book. Your input has been incredibly valuable and I am so grateful.

CONTENTS

ABOUT THE AUTHOR

Chris Janke-Bueno has been an athlete his entire life. At 13 years of age, he herniated a disc in his lower back. After trying several modalities, the solution to the pain was balancing exercises similar to what you find in this book.

For the last 15 years, he's been a personal trainer, helping others achieve their fitness goals without injuring themselves.

Chris is a passionate trainer, writer, and athlete.

He lives in San Jose, CA with his wife of 10 years and his four kids.

CONTACT

I hope you gain value from this book. For additional resources to help you manage your back pain, visit www.mycorebalance.com

E-mail questions and comments to chris@mycorebalance.com

For other books written by Chris Janke-Bueno, or for information on personal training programs,

visit www.mycorebalance.com

Why Does Your Back Hurt?

An Important Disclaimer

Back pain is the worst. It can completely take you away from the life you want to live. Sometimes you get major flare-ups, and sometimes the pain will just sort of linger in the background, but it always grabs your attention. Spasm, tightness, and numbness are all associated with this pain. The worst part can be the fear that it produces.

The first step to calming that fear is to know what's happening. It's valuable to know if you're dealing with something major like a herniated disc, stenosis, or scoliosis… or just some tight muscles. Talk to a doctor to rule out any serious conditions. Getting a diagnosis can be helpful and give you peace of mind. It allows you the freedom to approach the next step with options.

In my 15 years as a personal trainer, I have seen three types of people with back pain:

1. People who are incredibly fit, yet don't allow their body enough time to recover. They get "too much of a good thing" and overtrain their body, tax their nervous system, and produce back pain.
2. I've also seen people allow their body to atrophy, by living a sedentary lifestyle, avoiding activity that causes even minor discomfort, and generally just allowing "old age" to take its toll.
3. The third category is people who have traumatic accidents, such as on a bike or in a car.

If you've recently suffered a traumatic accident, put this book down for later. Talk to a doctor and begin to take the first steps toward healing. Then pick up this book again later when the time is right.

If you know you are dealing with muscle imbalances, tightness, and weakness, this book can help you to systematically strengthen, stretch, and balance your body. Use it as a tool, not a crutch. Let this book help you, but remember that the responsibility for your health is yours.

One final warning:

If you feel like there is something significantly wrong with your body, such as a broken bone, bulging disc, dislocation, etc. then put this book down and make sure you have taken the necessary action with a medical professional to get that checked out.

Activities That Could Exacerbate The Pain

Everyone has habits, the question is are they producing a strong back… or chronic pain?

As you begin using this book, remember that these daily exercises function in the context of the rest of your life. Make sure you have positive habits to support you in becoming pain-free.

Painful Activity #1 - Prolonged Sitting

We all sit too much. Our modern lifestyle does not provide us with the natural baseline movements that it takes to stay healthy.

Take movement breaks by setting a timer. Ideally, you'd work about 45 minutes and then take a 10 minute break.

Painful Activity #2 - The "No Pain No Gain" Fitness Philosophy

Your workout doesn't have to hurt to work!

When you're at the gym, your main focus should be on your form, not how much weight you're lifting. Stop when the repetitions are no longer at 100% quality form. It's better to stop a workout early than to sacrifice your form and throw out your back.

Painful Activity #3 - Exercise Inconsistency

Until you have established consistency of your workout program, your results will be limited. Injury can hamper progress, so approach progression carefully.

It's important to do *something* everyday. Commit to just 10 minutes at first, and then begin to add to that. Start with the goal of "perfect attendance" and pretty soon you'll be seeing results that you didn't before. Remember the quote: "half the battle is just showing up."

Painful Activity #4 - Overdoing Cardio

Running, biking, and other cardiovascular activities are great to condition your body and lose weight. The problem is when you overdo it. Here's a strategy to prevent this from happening.

Start with form as your focus, and then gradually add distance, speed, and time. For example, let's say you feel really good, so you start your 3-mile run. Your form is fantastic, and you're cruising along. After a mile at good pace, you start to slow down. You notice your form begins to suffer. At this point, you should stop. Even though you planned to do three miles, you're done. Stop. Take a day or two to rest, and then try again. Endurance will come after you establish quality of movement first. Don't try to develop endurance with bad form.

Painful Activity #5 - Poor Health in General

Poor health is not something you have, it's a habit you've created. Take pride and ownership of your health, no matter how bad it is now, then make a commitment now to turn this ship around. If you are overweight, I recommend focusing on proper nutrition first, and keeping the exercise light, like the exercises you'll find in this book. Once you've lost some weight and are feeling more confident, then you can begin to ramp up the intensity.

Painful Activity #6 - Poor Nutrition

Try to improve a little everyday. Start with this simple checklist:

1. Cut all beverages except water, drink ½ to 1 gallon of water per day.
2. Drink a green fruit / vegetable smoothie daily.
3. Cut packaged snacks, replace with fruits and vegetables.
4. Cut fried food, hydrogenated oils, and trans fats. And add healthy fats.
5. Cut out processed protein, and add natural protein.
6. Convert starchy carbs to green carbs.
7. Practice perfect proportions (divide your plate equally between protein, carbs, fat, and greens).

Painful Activity #7 - Not Enough Sleep

Most people don't sleep enough. With all our demands, it can be challenging to prioritize it.

Eight hours of sleep is the minimum. If you are exercising, your body needs time to repair itself from the vigors of fitness, so you may need even more. Slowly build up your sleep until you can wake up without an alarm clock. If you need coffee to wake up, you're not sleeping enough.

Implementing these healthy habits will help you create a solid foundation. Now, let's move on to the specific exercises.

WORKOUT #1
RELAX THE MUSCLES

Muscles can only do two things: work and rest. This first workout is teaching your body to relax.

Do these exercises daily for three to four weeks before you progress to the next workout. Follow the directions carefully. If you have questions, look up the exercises on the My Core Balance YouTube channel.

Static Back

Form

Lie on your back with your legs draped over a chair, ottoman, or large block.

Relax and breathe deeply.

Purpose

Relaxes the back, hips, and neck.

This is a great exercise to do at the start of a workout, or by itself after a long day.

Time

Do a minimum of five minutes, up to 30 minutes.

Strap Presses

Form

In Static Back Position, tie a strap just above your knees so your legs are 4 inches apart. Press

out on the strap, hold for two seconds, and then release the pressure. Repeat.

Purpose

Strengthens the outer hip muscles, which are important stabilizers.

Time

1 to 3 minutes.

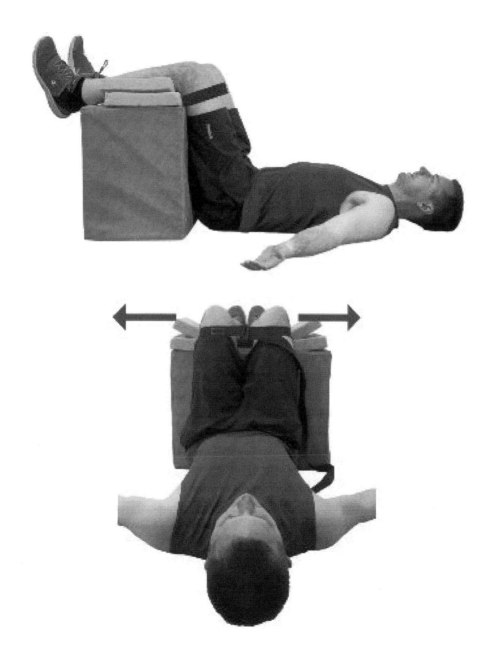

Pillow Squeezes

Form

In Static Back position, place a pillow between your knees, about 4 inches wide.

Squeeze the pillow with your knees, hold for two seconds, and then slowly release. Repeat.

Purpose

Activate and strengthen the adductors, or inner thighs.

These muscles are important pelvic stabilizers.

Time

1 to 3 minutes.

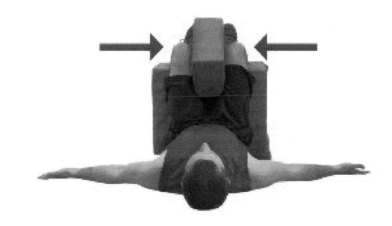

Reverse Presses

Form

In the Static Back position, bring your elbows up to shoulder level, and your hands above your elbows pointed toward the ceiling. Next, squeeze your shoulder blades toward each other and press your elbows into the floor. Hold for two seconds, then relax. You should feel the work in the upper back.

Purpose

Promotes healthy upper back and shoulder blade movement.

Strengthens the muscles that give you good posture,

which takes tension off the lower back.

Time

1 to 3 minutes.

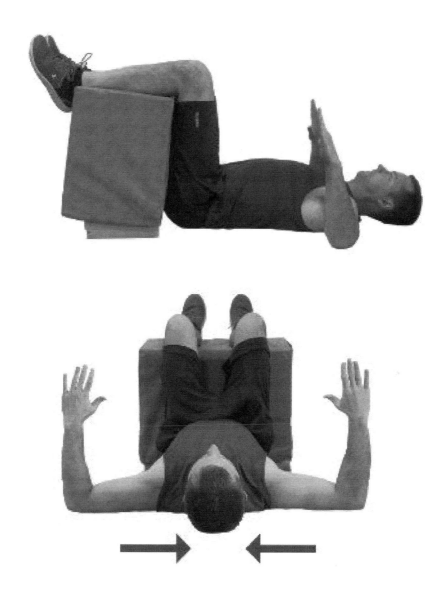

Goal Posts

Form

Begin in Reverse Press position. Next, rotate from the shoulder so that your hands go down toward the floor, overhead. Touch the floor if it's easy for you to do. If not, stop when you can't comfortably go any further. Then bring your hands back to starting position.

Purpose

Softens the shoulders through passive external rotation.

This is an under-used range of motion for most people. This exercise restores that movement safely.

Time

1 to 3 minutes.

Pullovers

Form

Hold a wooden bar above your chest with your hands about 2 feet wide.

Next, bring your hands down toward the floor, overhead, while holding the bar.

Then slowly return to the starting position.

Purpose

Relaxes the upper back and neck.

Restores overhead range of motion safely.

Relieves tension in the upper trapezius muscle.

Time

1 to 3 minutes.

Quad Stretch

Form

Lie face down. Bend one knee and hold onto that foot with your hand.

Engage your gluteal muscles tightly so that your hips press down into the floor.

Pull your heel toward your gluteal muscles on the same side. Hold.

Purpose

Stretch the quad muscle.

Helps to neutralize the pelvis,

which allows the lower back angle to neutralize.

Time

1 minute each side.

Hamstring Stretch

Form

Lie on your back with your legs up a wall. Tighten your thighs, and pull your toes down toward

you. Make sure your hips are flat on the floor. If your hips come up,

move away from the wall until they are flat. Hold the position.

Purpose

Stretches the hamstring and calves.

Helps stabilize the lower body,

therefore creating a more stable foundation for the spine.

Time

1 minute.

Groin Stretch

Form

Lie on your back with one leg over a chair and the other leg out straight.

Put a weighted object next to your extended leg, so your foot and leg do not fall out to the side.

Relax in this position.

Purpose

Relaxes the back, hips, and neck.

Helps to counteract the negative effects of sitting.

Elongates the psoas muscle, which in turn takes tension off the lower back.

Time

Do a minimum of five minutes, up to 30 minutes on each leg.

Cats and Dogs

Form

Start on your hands and knees. Alternate between the following positions:

CAT – breathe out as you tuck your hips under, round your back, and look down.

DOG – breathe in as you roll your hips to put an arch in your back, and look up.

Purpose

Takes the spine through a full range of motion.

Relaxes the hips, spine, shoulders, and neck.

Allows your breathing to regulate.

Time

1 to 3 minutes.

CHRIS JANKE-BUENO

WORKOUT #2
MOBILIZE THE JOINTS

Hopefully you've spent some time consistently doing Workout #1. Now, it's time to improve flexibility and range of motion.

Each joint in the body has an ideal range of motion that it's able to accomplish. Your ankles, knees, hips, spine, and shoulders each function in a different way. Improving flexibility and range of motion are important ways to achieve your goal of a pain-free back.

90-90 In-Out

Form

Begin on your back with your legs up in 90° angles at the hips and knees. Keep your abdominals

engaged so that your lower back stays flat on the floor. Touch your knees and ankles together.

Then bring your knees and ankles wide, keeping your shins parallel.

Next, slowly return to the starting position. Repeat.

Purpose

Strengthens the abs, hip flexors, and quads.

Opens up a lateral range of motion in the hips, while helping the upper back stay an extension.

Time

1 to 3 minutes.

Hip Circles

Form

Lie on your back with one leg out straight and the other one in the 90–90 position.

Circle your bent knee, so that you form circles around your hip.

Circle one direction, then switch directions. Repeat on the other leg.

Purpose

The hip is a ball and socket joint, and this exercise strengthens the surrounding muscles so that

the hips can function better with the ball and socket circular movement.

Time

30 seconds to 1 minute each direction, then repeat on the other side.

Hip Flexor Lifts

Form

Lie on your back with your knees bent and feet flat on the floor.

Keep your back flat as you bring a leg towards your chest, stopping at 90°.

Slowly lower, and repeat on the same side for the given time. Then switch sides and repeat.

Purpose

Strengthens the hip flexors, while also creating strength in the abs and obliques as they stabilize the core.

Time

1 minute each leg.

Snow Angels

Form

Lie on your back. Begin with your arms down at your side, and your palms down.

Slowly slide your arms up until your hands are at shoulder level, then rotate your arms so your palms face the ceiling. Next, continue the motion overhead until you are not able to comfortably go any further. Do not force the range of motion. Return by doing the same movement in the opposite direction. Repeat.

Purpose

This exercise takes the shoulders through their full range of motion. It also stretches the peripheral muscles such as the biceps.

Time

1 to 3 minutes.

Weighted Pullovers

Form

Begin on your back with your knees bent and feet flat on the floor. Hold a weight in front of your chest, keeping your elbows straight. Bring your hands overhead toward the floor, without forcing the movement. Keep your back flat by bracing with your abs. Return to the starting position.

Purpose

Strengthens and stretches the shoulders and lats.

Helps to stabilize the back by bracing with the abdominal and oblique muscles.

Time

1 minute.

Shoulder Rolls

Form

Stand with your feet straight ahead.

Softly roll your shoulders forward, hitting all points in the range of motion.

Repeat backwards.

Purpose

Strengthens your shoulder muscles.

Stabilizes your shoulder blades and upper back.

Increases range of motion.

Time

30 seconds to 1 minute forwards.

30 seconds to 1 minute backwards.

Upper Spinal Floor Twist

Form

Lie on your side with your knees and hips at 90° angles and your hands together in front of you.

Next, take your top hand and open your body like a book. Relax your upper body and just let

gravity take you down. Keep your knees lined up. Breathe slowly and deeply. Hold.

Purpose

Increases the torso range of motion through passive relaxation.

Improves stability of the lower body. Helps to calm your breathing.

Time

1 to 3 minutes on each side.

Cats and Dogs

Form

Start on your hands and knees. Alternate between the following two positions:

CAT – breathe out as you tuck your hips under, round your back, and look down.

DOG – breathe in as you roll your hips to put an arch in the back, and look up.

Purpose

Takes the spine through a full range of motion.

Relaxes the hips, spine, shoulders, and neck.

Allows your breathing to regulate.

Time

1 to 3 minutes.

Prone Arm Raises

Form

Lying face down, bring your hands down by your hips. Next, use your upper back muscles to pull your shoulder blades together and lift your shoulders away from the floor. Then lift up the hands. Lower down and repeat.

Purpose

Strengthens the upper back and improves the range of motion of the shoulder blades.

Stretches the front of the shoulder and chest.

Time

1 minute.

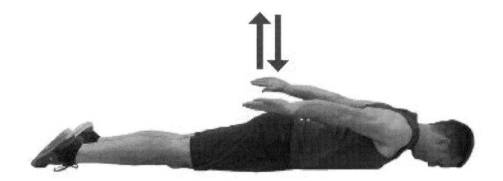

Foot Circles

Form

Lie on your back and lift one leg up. Keep that leg is straight as you can at the knee. Circle the foot and ankle clockwise, then counterclockwise. Then make a straight line up-and-down (point and flex). Repeat on the other foot.

Purpose

Helps to balance the musculature of the lower leg.

Can improve balance and proprioception

(your ability to feel your body in space).

Time

20 repetitions right, 20 repetitions left, and 20 repetitions point-flex.

Then repeat on the other foot.

CHRIS JANKE-BUENO

WORKOUT #3
STABILIZE THE JOINTS

Congratulations on making it this far!

By now, you should have 2 to 4 weeks of workout #1 done daily. Then another 2 to 4 weeks of workout #2. Now you're ready to stabilize what you've done. Stability is important for keeping away your back pain.

Do this workout every other day, and on the alternating days add in one of the previous two workouts. For example, Monday is workout #3, Tuesday is workout #1, Wednesday is work #3 again, Thursday is workout #2, etc.

Repeat that pattern for 2 to 6 weeks.

Outer Thighs

Form

Lie on your side with your legs straight. Lift one leg up to the side, keeping it straight.

Slightly internally rotate your top leg, so that the kneecap points slightly down.

Once you reach the top of your range of motion, slowly lower back down and repeat.

Purpose

Strengthens the outer hip and thigh.

Creates stability by forcing the body to stabilize during the movement.

Time

1 minute each leg.

Inner Thigh

Form

Lie on your side, then bring your top leg forward and rest the foot on the floor with the knee up.

Tighten up the thigh on the straight (bottom) leg. Next, lift the bottom leg off the floor slightly,

then lower down slowly. Repeat.

Purpose

Strengthens the inner thigh.

Improves overall pelvic stability, leading to better spinal stability.

Time

1 minute each leg.

Leg Raises

Form

Lie on your back with your knees bent and your feet flat on the floor.

Straighten the left leg. Flex the left ankle and pull the toes back toward you.

Lift the left leg up until the knees are touching, then lower back down. Repeat for the entire set,

and then repeat on the right side.

Purpose

Strengthens the hip flexor and quad.

Time

1 minute each leg.

Donkey Kicks

Form

Begin on your hands and knees.

Lift one leg behind you so that the foot points up to the ceiling.

Slowly lower back down towards the starting position. Repeat.

Purpose

Strengthens the glutes and hamstrings.

Creates more core stability.

Indirectly stretches the front of the hip and leg.

Time

1 minute each leg.

Quad Stretch - No Hands

Form

Lie face down. Engage your abs and your glutes. Rotate your hips and flatten your lower back.

Bend one knee and bring the heel toward your hips. Keep your hamstring engaged.

Hold the position. Repeat on the other leg.

Purpose

Strengthens the hamstrings.

Stretches the quads.

Neutralizes the pelvic tilt.

Time

1 minute each leg.

Spread Foot Forward Bend

Form

Stand with your feet wide and toes pointed straight ahead. Keep your thighs tight and your legs straight. Next, lean forward, keeping your back straight. Hold. Then walk your hands to the right foot and hold, then the left foot and hold, and lastly back to the middle for one last hold.

Purpose

Stretches the hamstrings.

Indirectly strengthens the quads,

and stabilizes the pelvis. Also stretches the ribs.

Time

15 to 30 seconds at each position

(front, left, right, then front again).

Lateral Raises

Form

Stand with your back against the wall. Keep your arms straight. Slide your arms up the wall,

keeping your pinky fingers touching the wall. At shoulder level, rotate your palms up. Continue

over your head, keeping your thumbs touching the wall. Lower down and repeat.

Purpose

Strengthens the shoulders

through a full range of motion.

Strengthens and stretches the rotator cuff.

Time

1 to 3 sets of one minute each.

Standing Pullovers

Form

Stand with your back against a wall. Hold onto a bar, strap, or belt.

Keep your elbows straight as you raise your hands overhead.

Lower down and repeat.

Purpose

Strengthens the shoulders and traps.

Opens up the overhead range of motion.

Great for posture of the upper back.

Time

1 to 3 sets of one minute each.

Standing Rotator Cuff

Form

Stand at a wall. Bend your elbows to 90°, with your elbows touching your ribs and the wall.

Next, bring your hands apart, keeping your elbows tucked in tightly. Reach your wrists toward

the wall. Hold.

Purpose

Sets your shoulder blades, upper back, and upper arms in the correct posture.

Stretches the chest and front of the shoulder.

Time

1 to 3 sets of one minute each.

Wall Sit

Form

Sit in an "imaginary chair" against the wall. Press your lower back flat into the wall. Keep your

weight in your heels, even lifting up your toes slightly.

Push into the heels like you're trying to move the floor away from you. Hold.

Purpose

Strengthens the quads in a balanced way, preventing your pelvis from rotating. This exercise

also balances the lower body and pelvis.

Time

30 seconds to 2 minutes.

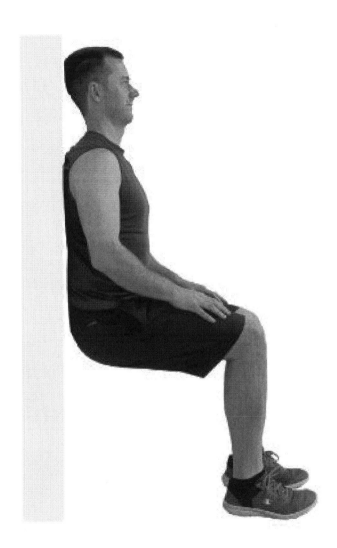

WORKOUT #4
STRENGTHEN THE MUSCLES

Here we are, at the strength building program. Because the intensity is higher in this workout, ease into it slowly. Make sure form is still your #1 priority. After all, we want to remain pain-free as we build up our strength.

To incorporate this workout into your routine, you can do a simple rotation. Do each workout in order:

- Day one is workout #1.
- Day two is workout #2.
- Day three is workout #3.
- Day four is workout #4.
- Then repeat.

90-90 with 2 Pillows

Form

Begin on your back. Place a pillow between your knees and one between your ankles.

Then lift your knees up toward you, so that your hips and knees are 90°.

Engage your abs to flatten your lower back. Hold.

Purpose

Strengthens the abdominals, hip flexors, and inner thighs.

Stabilizes the pelvis and lower back.

Time

1 minute.

Hands and Knees Elbow Curls

Form

Curl your fingers into the palm of your hand and put your knuckles on your temples with your thumb pointing toward your shoulders. From the starting position, slowly bring your elbow up toward the ceiling, and then back down so that it touches the inside of the other elbow. Simultaneously, as you bring the elbow away from the midline, you also want to bring the opposite knee away from the midline. Repeat.

Purpose

Full body strength and stability of your hips, shoulders, and core.

Time

1 minute each side.

1

2

Bird-Dog

Form

Begin on your hands and knees. Next, point one arm forward and the opposite leg back.

You want to create a straight line from your fingertips to your toes.

Hold. Then repeat on the other side.

Purpose

Full body stabilization:

hips, shoulders, and core.

Also promotes hip extension.

Time

1 minute each side.

Twist Plank

Form

Begin with both hands on the floor with arms straight. Stack your feet on top of each other. Your

upper body is in the front plank, and your lower body is in a side plank. Hold.

Purpose

Full body stabilization.

Shoulder strength.

Oblique strength.

Time

15 seconds to 1 minute on each side.

Overhead Wall Squat

Form

Start in a basic Wall Sit position. Next, bring your feet and knees wide. Make sure your feet and knees are pointing in the same direction. Bring your back off the wall, so the only thing touching the wall is your glutes. Grip a pole or belt and bring your hands overhead. Hold.

Purpose

Quad strength. Back strength.

Shoulder strength.

Time

15 seconds to 2 minutes.

Superman

Form

Lie face down on the floor with your legs straight and your arms stretched out overhead.

Raise your upper body and legs off the floor as if you're flying like Superman.

Hold this position briefly then lower yourself back down to the floor. Repeat.

Purpose

Back strength.

Glute strength.

Full body extension.

Time

Hold 15 seconds to 2 minutes.

Pullovers with Leg Raises

Form

Begin on your back with your knees and hips at 90° angles. Hold on to a pole in front of your chest, keeping your elbows straight. Bring your hands to the floor, without forcing the movement. At the same time, bring your feet toward the floor while keeping your knees at 90° angles. Return to the starting position. Repeat.

Purpose

Strengthens the abdominals in order to protect the lower back.

Time

1 to 3 sets of 1 minute each.

Table Top

Form

Begin by sitting on the floor with your hands positioned behind you. Raise your hips up so that your hips, knees, and shoulders are lined up together. Engage your upper back so your shoulder blades pinch toward each other. Hold.

Purpose

Shoulder flexibility.

Back extension.

Hip extension.

Time

1 minute.

Windmill

Form

Stand with your back against the wall, with your thighs tight. Bring your arms out to the side

against the wall with your palms facing forward. Flex your spine to the side, then return to the

middle, then go to the other side. Keep your shoulders touching the wall and your heels touching

the floor. Repeat.

Purpose

Flexibility of the ribs and shoulders.

Foundational stability of the hips and legs.

Time

15 seconds to 2 minutes.

SUCCESS STORIES

Nancy was in her 50's when she came to see me because she had hip pain. She showed me her x-ray, and I cringed just looking at it. The top of her femur (thigh bone) was jammed into the hip socket, with none of the necessary joint space to allow for good movement. The cartilage was gone. One bone was literally rubbing against the other.

We began working together. Over the next year, Nancy dedicated herself to the exercises. She and I met once per week and she also did the exercises daily at home.

A year later, she got another x-ray. I wasn't surprised that she now had space between her bones. After all, she had been very disciplined. Her muscles had become strong and balanced enough so that they were able to hold her bones in the right position. However, I was pleasantly surprised with what was in the space between the bones.

"What is that white stuff?" I asked.

"Cartilage," she replied. "I have new cartilage growth."

It wasn't fully formed, but sure enough there were little wisps of cartilage growth.

A flood of thoughts swarmed my head. *Amazing! The human body is truly amazing! Did the exercises grow the cartilage? Of course not. But the exercises helped to re-balance the muscles, which helped create joint space by moving the bones into the right alignment. Once there was joint space, the body grew cartilage.*

The human body has the incredible capability to regenerate itself. When we give the body the right raw materials and put it in the right condition to thrive, the body regenerates until the day we die. Those right conditions are

- well-rounded balancing exercises,
- adequate sleep,
- stress coping mechanisms,
- full deep breathing,
- adequate hydration,
- proper nutrition,
- healthy relationships,
- connection to nature,
- and an overall purpose for living.

When all of these components are in proper balance, we have a body that is healthy, strong, and pain-free.

In Their Own Words

Amor:

When I first started, I didn't have any specific pain. I was just out of alignment and definitely needed to be stronger and healthier.

Then, in 2016, I was diagnosed with ovarian cancer and had to stop my workouts. I resumed workouts one month after my last chemotherapy session. I was quite weak and really out of alignment. I could barely hold any of the basic positions. My posture was stooped; I had rounded shoulders and a bit of a humped back.

Due to chemotherapy, I developed osteopenia and had difficulty moving my shoulders and upper arms. It was very painful to stretch them out and up, as well as place them behind my back - simple movements that I used to do all the time prior to cancer treatment.

I also had trouble with my legs and feet, especially in getting up from a seated position. On top of that, I fell a couple of times due to imbalance and weak ankles.

I have one hour sessions with Chris twice a week (every Monday and Thursday).

My experience with My Core Balance has been nothing short of wonderful! I have gained so much strength, my body is well-aligned, and the areas of concern I had before have diminished considerably if not disappeared altogether.

Engaging with my trainer Chris is what I enjoy most during my workouts. I continue learning about the muscles in my body, especially about how the workout he's giving me is related to their function and strength. When it comes to my body's movements and the exercises/positions he instructs me to hold, it's important for me to understand what I am doing and why.

There is so much value in what and how Chris trains me because, not only is he technically knowledgeable on how the body works, he constantly (and patiently) guides me on how to do the exercises/positions correctly, e.g. what muscles to focus on and why. He's very open to questions and formulates the answers in ways that I can understand e.g. analogies, examples, pictures. When it comes to his jokes, they're … uhmm … okay.

I'm not completely pain-free per se, as my body is still dealing with the side effects from my cancer treatment. Nevertheless, I am able to inform Chris whenever something arises, and he immediately (and patiently) adjusts my workouts accordingly.

Leo:

Prior to joining My Core Balance, I had chronic back pain that lasted for more than a year. On the early stages, the pain was so bad I couldn't sleep for more than 4 - 5 hours a day. I always woke up having a terrible pain, that forced me to walk around for a minimum of 30 minutes before I could even lay back down on the bed.

I had a lot of medical tests prior to focusing myself on fixing body posture, as I wasn't convinced that my problem was due to the 'lack of exercise and bad posture.' However, after a lot of physical therapy sessions, medical checkups, even MRIs, and not finding any issues, even my doctor was starting to attribute the issues to the bad physical training and not an underlying medical issue.

My first few sessions with Chris were a true eye-opener, as at that point, I saw how bad my posture was, and how weak my core and critical muscles were. Even with only a once-per-week sessions, I could feel that my back pain started to disappear after a while, and that's without a 'no pain no gain' attitude that I was used to getting in a personal training session.

The sessions with Chris not only helped to improve important muscles, create better habits, but also help with the most critical part, awareness of where things were wrong, and that, in my experience, is always an important start to something good. I do fall back to bad habits (and ignorance) time and again, and my back will start to be stiff if I do, so I have a good natural reminder to always keep myself on Chris' work-out regime.

Sue:

I have suffered with back pain ever since I was a teenager. I have found temporary relief through chiropractors, massage, acupuncture and physical therapy. It wasn't until I met Chris that I finally got lasting relief from my back pain. His exercises are simple and effective.

After working with Chris, I know how to take care of my back. On a daily basis, my back feels great, and I know what to do if my back starts to hurt for any reason. Recently, I tripped and felt the impact throughout my body. I did some of Chris's exercise, went to bed early and woke up feeling fine the next day.

I recommend Chris's routines for anyone who wants to have a stronger back!

YOU!
Send me *your* success story to chris@mycorebalance.com.

NOW WHAT? LIFE AFTER THE PROGRAM

If you followed the directions of this book, you have spent the last several months doing these four workouts. These workouts will continue to be your foundation of stability and strength for the rest of your life.

Keep these four workouts in your back pocket, and use them as "recovery days" or warm-ups for harder workouts.

Do what you love, decide what inspires you and go for it.

This is not the end, but the beginning. Reach out to me if there's anything else I can help you with.

"Let's be fit. Let's be healthy. Let's be happy. It feels good to move, so keep moving."

In Health,

Chris Janke-Bueno

HELP!
I THREW OUT MY BACK

Four Workouts to Ease Muscle Tension and Develop Core Strength

Back pain can often be helped with gentle exercises and stretches. This book can help you to systematically strengthen, stretch, and balance your body. There are four total workouts in this book, each directed toward the ultimate goal of pain-free movement. Each workout consists of just 10 simple exercises that you can do at home, work, or on the road:

1. **The first workout's goal is to relax the muscles.**

2. **The second workout's goal is to mobilize the joints through a full range of motion.**

3. **The third workout's goal is to stabilize the joints.**

4. **The fourth workout's goal is to strengthen the muscles.**

This book is for someone who wants to take control of their back pain without having to resort to surgery, medication, or manipulation. It includes pictures with simple descriptions, and is suitable for beginner exercisers.

The workouts always feel great - I always say that I feel like I got a massage afterwards. —BETSY HICKS

CHRIS JANKE-BUENO has been an athlete his whole life. A back injury and subsequent healing fueled his desire to help others live a pain-free, active life.

He enjoys teaching, training, writing, and speaking about healthy principles.

He lives in San Jose, California, with his wife and four kids.

Photography by Alison Williams